Monika Wegler

Dogs

**How to Take Care of Them
and Understand Them**

With color photographs
by Monika Wegler
and drawings by
György Jankovics

Consulting Editor:
Matthew M. Vriends, Ph.D.

BARRON'S

Contents

Preceding double spread: *A chow chow and a Bernese mountain dog are the parents of this mongrel. It is four months old.*
Drawing, right: *A dachshund sits up and begs.*

Preface

You bring a dog into your house with the intention of having it become a member of the household. It takes some time, however, for dogs and humans to understand each other well enough to have what one could term a happy relationship. Because mistakes made during this adjustment phase can be difficult to correct later, all dog lovers need to know how to take proper care of their pets from the outset.

In this Barron's Pet Owner's Manual, author Monika Wegler explains, step by step, everything that a dog needs to become a confident, obedient animal. This learning program is designed in such a way that owners and their pets will enjoy it equally.

The pictures and instructions provided on the How-To pages deal with other aspects of keeping a dog successfully: housebreaking—an important issue—daily care, proper nutrition, rules for keeping your pet healthy, and—not least of all—learning to understand how dogs communicate.

Anyone who is about to buy a dog can use the puppy test (see page 8) to become better acquainted with the puppy's disposition before making the purchase.

Expert advice, informative drawings, and excellent color photos—all taken by the author—make this book an indispensable companion for all dog owners.

The author of this book and the editors of Barron's series of nature books wish you much pleasure with your dog.

Your dog, your best friend— but friendship has to be earned. The way to earn it is through loving, but firm training, proper feeding, and an understanding of the behavior patterns of your four-legged friend, which, after all, is descended from the wolf.

Please read the "Important Note" on page 63.

Before Buying a Dog

Is There Room for a Dog in Your Life?

Centuries of domestication have molded the dog's distinctive nature and fixed its attention on human beings. Its owner is all a dog has: provider, pack leader, family. Anyone who makes a dog part of his or her life needs to be aware of the following: Dogs are costly in terms of effort, time, and money; they have to be trained lovingly and cared for so that they have a sense of well-being. For this to be possible, owners have to know what dogs expect from humans, and what they themselves can expect from their pets. Only in this way can the beautiful, unique relationship between human and dog have a chance to develop.

These issues are also important:
- Are you prepared to devote two to three hours per day to your pet for 10 to 15 years? (dogs can live this long)
- Is keeping a dog compatible with your professional situation and family life? A dog should not be left alone for more than four hours per day.
- Who will take care of the dog if you are ill?
- Can you afford a dog? Accessories, food, veterinary expenses, license, and insurance cost (depending on the breed) $500 to $1,000 or more annually.
- Will your landlord permit you to keep a dog in your apartment?
- Are all the family members in agreement with the purchase of a dog?

A boxer, six weeks old—a lovable, high-spirited family pet, it has to be trained with firmness and a great deal of praise.

A child's wish alone should not be the determining factor in the acquisition of a dog.
- Is any member of the family allergic to dog hair? If in doubt, consult your physician before buying a dog.

Which Dog Is Right for You?

The numerous breeds of dogs, or their mixtures, differ not only in appearance, but also—quite markedly—in characteristics and temperament. For this reason, the following considerations are important.

Purebred or Mongrel?

It is absolutely necessary to obtain precise information about a pedigreed dog or, in the case of a mongrel, to get some idea of a dog's parentage.

Mongrels: There are about 400 breeds of dogs; nevertheless, many dog lovers decide to keep a mongrel or mutt as a pet. Their main argument, apart from the low price, is this: "Mongrels are more intelligent, healthier, and better-natured." This may or may not be true; mongrels also can develop inherited diseases or possess latent traits that later prove troublesome. If you do not know a mongrel's parents, there may be unpleasant surprises.

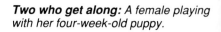

Two who get along: *A female playing with her four-week-old puppy.*

A chewing bone made of buffalo hide and a hard rubber ring are ideal playthings for dogs.

Purebred dogs: Here you have a better idea of what to expect: The appearance and characteristics have been molded for generations by selective breeding. Be sure to find out everything possible about the purpose for which the breed originally was bred and used, because this continues to influence the dog's nature and needs. The dachshund, for example, originally was bred for hunting. It is still used as a hunting dog, of course, but it also is one of the more popular family dogs. As a hunter, its task is to crawl into a badger's burrow or a fox hole—for this purpose it needs the qualities of courage and independence. Willfulness, which is among the little animal's most prominent characteristics, certainly is related to these character traits. It is precisely this quality that causes problems for so many dachshund owners when training their pets. Take this into account too: In selective breeding, beauty and exotic breed characteristics are often the most important criteria; to obtain them, breeders will even accept impaired health as part of the bargain. As a result, hip joint problems (hip dysplasia) or eye diseases are preprogrammed in some breeds.

Important: Whether you choose a purebred or a mongrel, consider what characteristics are particularly important to you. Is the dog intended to be a patient playmate for children, an untiring companion on biking trips, or a cute lap dog? Find out (from the puppy's owner, a breed club, or specialized books) whether the dog really has the characteristics you expect.

You also need to know that not every small dog is a gentle little lap dog. The Yorkshire terrier, a former rat catcher, has an especially dominant nature, and this "half-pint" needs training just as firm as that of a large dog.

Tip: The larger the dog, the more space it demands and—usually—the more exercise it needs. To keep a Great Dane or an Afghan in a one-room apartment is cruel to the animal.

Female or Male?

Females generally are believed to be more affectionate and more easily trained than males. Heat, or estrus, which occurs approximately every six months (see page 54), is a problem for many dog owners. Because all the males in the entire neighborhood display their undisguised interest at this time, walks often become an ordeal, as it is necessary to prevent an unwanted pregnancy. These problems can be avoided by spaying the dog (see page 55).

Males are more combative than females because they want to stand their ground against other males. Once they have the scent of a female in heat, nothing will keep them from trying to reach the object of their interest.

Where to Get Your Dog

In a pet store or in the pet departments of large department stores. A good pet store owner will provide information about the litter, advise you, and help you procure a healthy dog.

From a breeder: You can obtain addresses from the Kennel Club (see page 60).

From amateur breeders and dog owners who do not belong to an association. Various puppies are usually advertised in newspapers. Look into these offers very carefully.

In animal shelters and from private societies for the prevention of cruelty to animals. Deciding to choose a dog here is laudable—but the longer the dog has lived in the shelter and the older the animal is, the more difficult it can be to adjust to a new home. A great deal of experience with dogs, much love, and patience are necessary here.

Do not buy from kennels that offer many breeds simultaneously, that cannot show you the puppy's mother, or that give only vague information about the origin of the dogs.

Choosing the Right Puppy

A puppy's charm is irresistible! Do not let yourself be guided solely by your emotions, however; be critical and take note of the following:

This is the correct way to pick up puppies and small dogs: Put one hand under the front paws and use the other to support the animal's rear.

How and where the puppy grows up: Today, owing to behavioral research, it is known that the first 12 weeks of life are decisive for a dog's development. If possible, take a look at the environment in which the puppy is growing up and observe the animal's contact with human beings. A dog that spends its youth exclusively in a pen and has no experience—or perhaps bad experiences—with humans will probably remain shy, fearful, and mistrustful. A good breeder gives the puppies lots of contact with humans. Anyone who wants a family pet has to make sure that the pup has become accustomed to children and visitors. In this way, while still young, the puppy becomes comfortable with the noise level customary in everyday family life and learns, for example, that it has no need to fear a humming vacuum cleaner.

Important: When buying from a breeder, choose your puppy early and make frequent visits to the mother and her litter to observe the little creature's development (see Puppy Test, pages 8 and 9).

The parents: The mother dog, or dam, should have a friendly, even disposition. If you can find out something about the father, so much the better.

Whether the puppy is healthy can be determined in this way:
• The coat is thick and shiny, with no bare patches, scabs, or parasites.
• The eyes are bright and not festering or watery.
• The anus is not smeared with feces.
• The ears are clean and not encrusted.
• The body is well-proportioned, not too lean, not too fat—a tightly filled little belly is normal after a puppy has eaten.

All puppies are adorable, sweet, and downright cuddly, but when buying a dog, do not be guided solely by your feelings. The more you know about the puppy's origin and development, the less trouble and disappointment you will experience.

7

How-To:
Puppy Test

Most appropriate for beginners is an even-tempered, well-balanced dog that is neither overly anxious nor too boisterous and aggressive. This test, intended to be fun for you and the puppy, is designed to help you find a dog that seems apt to develop into a pet with a healthy measure of self-confidence, easy to get along with and easy to train.

Important: In using this test, keep in mind the animal's frame of mind. The puppy may be about to eat or fall asleep, or it may not be in the mood to participate.

Test 1: Watch the Puppy in the Litter

Visit your future pet frequently, and use this test to track the dog's development.

Sit down quietly and watch how the puppies deal with each

Dachshunds with an air of innocence.

other. Behavior such as nipping and biting each other indicates nothing negative about their nature; on the contrary, it is an important part of their development. Through games involving scuffling and tussling, dogs practice getting along with one another. In this process, they learn, for example, that biting causes pain, and that howling

is a signal to let go. Only in this way do they learn to curb the inclination to bite.

Watch to see who is the leader of the pack. Later, this dog also will try to stand its ground against you. At the opposite pole is the runt, present in almost every litter. The runt usually keeps itself aloof and appears fearful; often it seems to be physically underdeveloped for its age. As a first-time dog owner, you should choose neither the leader nor the runt. A great deal of experience with dogs is necessary to succeed in correcting the extreme behavior of a leader or a runt. Love alone is not enough.

Test 2: See How They React to Humans

Do not attempt this test until the puppies are at least four weeks old. Go up to the young dogs; if the little creatures draw back in fright, they have had bad experiences with human beings. It is not so easy to gain the trust of such dogs.

The puppy should approach curiously when beckoned.

It is a good sign if the puppies take a wait-and-see attitude or even display curiosity. If this happens, proceed to the next step. Squat and call the dogs in a soft voice. Puppies that have developed in a healthy fashion will rush up to you and greet you. Usually, the leader of the pack will be out in front, whereas the more timid puppies approach more or less hesitantly.

Test 3: Observe a Single Puppy

This test is appropriate once the puppies are six weeks old. Remove the puppy you have chosen—after watching the litter as a whole and seeing the animals' reaction to you—from the pack and take it to a room that is new to it. Do not show any attention to the dog; just give it plenty of time. If it explores the room curiously, it is engaging in healthy behavior. If it stays fearfully in its place or crawls into a corner, this dog probably will continue to approach new situations hesitantly and anxiously.

Test 4: Call the Puppy to You

Make this test right after Test 3. After watching the puppy for a while, try to get it to come to you. Squat, click your tongue, call the puppy, and gently pat the floor with your hand. If it comes rushing up, this is a good sign. Later, this dog will participate freely and inquisitively in its training. A disinterested, timid puppy will be harder to teach.

Test 5: Test the Puppy's Playfulness

If the puppy is not tired after Tests 3 and 4, continue with this step; otherwise, postpone it to another day. Take a ball and try to arouse the dog's interest by calling it and showing it the ball. As soon as the puppy shows interest, roll the ball past it along the floor. A dog whose development is normal will run inquisitively after this "prey." If the animal shows no reaction to the ball, the breeder may have neglected to play with it or to try to initiate games. It may, however, also be an indication of a behavioral peculiarity.

Tip: See whether the puppy wants to participate in further testing. Don't push it too hard! It is not important for the puppy to finish the entire test sequence in one attempt; it is the individual reactions that matter.

Test 6: See the Puppy's Reaction to Noises

You are alone in a room with the puppy. Clap your hands loudly. If it looks inquiringly toward the source of the noise, this is an indication of a steady disposition. If the animal flinches or runs away in a panic, it will later flee from everyday noises. With some degree of

certainty, this puppy may be described as fearful.

Taking the Puppy Home

During the drive home, it is best to let the puppy ride in a small box with a blanket on the bottom. Take someone with you so that one of you can hold the box and keep the puppy calm. If the drive is a long one, take along your pet's collar and leash, because you will have to take breaks to let the dog relieve itself. While it is doing so, make sure to keep it on the leash; otherwise, the puppy might run away in fear and terror, at astonishing speed.

This healthy puppy is not timid about exploring a purse.

Everything a Dog Needs

Before picking up your new house-mate, get everything the dog will require for the first few days. In this way you will avoid frantic shopping and wrong purchases.

Shopping List

Before the dog enters your house, shop for the items it requires:
- One food dish and one water dish
- Puppy foods
- Leash and collar
- Blanket or basket
- Toys
- Comb and brush
- Address capsule or name tag

Once the dog is living in your house, it needs the following:
- Insurance
- Tattoo
- Vaccination record (usually obtainable from the previous owner)
- Possibly a dog whistle

Food and Water Dishes

Every dog needs its own dishes—a set of two, to be precise: a bowl for water—fresh water always has to be available—and a food dish. For water, I recommend a bowl made of glazed clay. For food, a high-grade steel dish with an antiskid rubber rim on the bottom is advisable. For dogs with particularly long ears (basset hound,

spaniel), there are special bowls that are narrower at the top to keep the dog's ears from drooping into its food when it eats. Plastic bowls are not recommended, because dogs overturn them, chew on them, and drag them around.

Puppy Foods

To determine the puppy's diet in the first few days, it is a good idea to ask the person who raised the puppy what it was fed. Even better, ask to take along some of its customary food for the initial period. In this way, serious difficulties in adjustment, such as diarrhea and vomiting, can be avoided. Special puppy chow is readily available commercially. (See also pages 36–41 for detailed information on feeding.)

Leash and Collar

A simple leather collar and a light leash, or lead, will be sufficient for your puppy at the outset, but remember that it soon will outgrow this basic equipment. For grown dogs, especially for relatively large and lively animals, I recommend so-called training collars with limited play (see Using the Leash Properly, page 23). These collars tighten when the dog tugs, but a guard prevents the chain from becoming too tight and cutting off the animal's air supply. The use of choke collars and collars with spikes, or spurs, borders on cruelty to animals.

Your dog needs more than a name to feel at home in your house; it needs all kinds of objects as well, including food and water dishes, a blanket, toys, a collar and leash, an address capsule or name tag, and a tattoo.

For certain breeds (such as the chow chow) or for small dogs, a chest harness (ask the breeder) is advisable.

In buying a leash, it is a matter of personal preference whether you choose a chain leash (waterproof) or a leather leash. The leashes with a spring that roll up automatically are quite practical. About 16' 5" (5 m) long, they give the dog some freedom of movement, yet still keep it safely leashed.

Blanket and Basket

Every dog needs a place that belongs to it exclusively, a little spot to which it can retreat. This need not be a basket; a thick blanket, a mattress, or a box will serve the same purpose. It is important that the dog lie so that it is not exposed to drafty air or a cold floor and so that it has enough room to stretch out on its bed.

Small dogs in particular feel safe and sheltered in this type of cozy dog igloo. Various models are sold in pet stores.

Small dogs like a roof over their heads. They show a preference for snug dog igloos (drawing, below) in which they feel safe and protected.

For medium-sized and small dogs, plastic pans, or trays, of the appropriate size are most practical.

Pretty to look at, but not recommended, are wicker baskets. Dogs gnaw on them, and they are difficult to clean.

The padding for a dog's bed has to be washable, warm, and cozy. You can use an ordinary blanket or a commercially available dog blanket and pads for dog baskets (ask whether everything is washable).

The Right Toys

These basic rules apply: A toy may not be so small that it can be swallowed; it may not have sharp edges; and it may not be made of materials that could prove harmful to the animal. Special chewing bones, hard rubber rings, cloth rags to shake, all kinds of balls, and—on walks—a stick of wood to throw (see Throwing balls and sticks, page 28) are ideal.

Comb and Brush

All dogs must have their coat groomed regularly. The types of combs and brushes you need will depend on your pet's coat (see Coat Care, page 42).

Address Capsule and Name Tag

Pet stores carry screw-top capsules that hold a piece of paper with room for the dog's name and the owner's telephone number. These capsules, however, come open easily, and then the slip of paper is lost. A better method is to seal the threads with nail polish.

This training collar tightens when there is a tug on the leash, but does not strangle the dog.

11

Apricot and black-and-tan Chihuahuas

Male Pekinese, one year old

V ery tiny, small, and medium-sized dogs are popular, including the Chihuahua, Yorkshire terrier, dachshund, poodle, basset hound, and other breeds pictured in the accompanying photos. Each one of them will be a lovable family pet—if you keep in mind that even the tiniest dog is a real dog and has to be trained just as lovingly and firmly as the larger members of the species.

Yorkshire terrier

Fox terrier dam with her puppy, nine weeks old

Cocker spaniels

Gray-and-white Shih Tzu and gold-and-white Shih Tzu

Tricolored basset hounds

Standard schnauzer

West Highland white terrier

Tricolored beagle

Long-haired dachshund and wire-haired dachshund

Toy poodle and miniature poodle

If the capsule does not appeal to you, have a small tag engraved and fasten it to the collar. Either a capsule or a tag is advisable. If your dog runs away, you can be informed quickly of its whereabouts.

Dog Whistle

If you would like to let your pet run free for longer distances on occasion, you can get it accustomed to an ultrasonic whistle, audible for your dog, but not for the human ear. You can spare yourself—and others—the trouble of repeated calling.

Vaccination Record

Because dogs are vaccinated for the first time when they are eight or nine weeks old, your pet probably will already have a vaccination record when it enters your care. Fill in your address and the dog's name, and take the document with you to the veterinarian's office. All inoculations are recorded. This record is indispensable for traveling abroad, because most countries admit only animals that have proof of vaccination against rabies.

Insurance

Even if the damage done by a small dog is limited, I recommend that you take out a dog liability insurance policy. Just imagine: If your pet breaks loose and causes an accident, the costs you incur can be vast.

Important: You are obligated to supervise your dog. The insurance company will have to pay only if you have performed your duty of supervision.

Tattoo

Purebred puppies usually are tattooed in the groin area or on the inside of the ear. Use either the dog's AKC registration number or your social security number. In this way, the animal's identity—according to its pedigree—is clearly established. If your pet is not yet tattooed, the veterinarian will perform this service. He also can tell you at what age your pet should be tattooed. A tattoo is more than a calling card for your purebred; it also will protect the dog. If your pet runs away or is stolen and ends up in an experimental lab, you will have a substantially greater chance of getting the animal back.

The tattoo in the ear aids in quick identification of runaway or stolen dogs.

A dog always should wear an address capsule or a name tag.

Acclimation and Training

The First Days at Home

Home at last! Now your dog needs time to look around and sniff everything in peace and quiet. According to its temperament, it will explore its future home either inquisitively and boldly or cautiously and timidly. Show your pet all the rooms that it will be allowed to enter, the places where it will eat and sleep, and the backyard, if you have one. Don't overdo it, however—an excessively loud, boisterous welcome by children, friends, and relatives would only frighten the dog. Once the initial excitement has subsided, it is time to eat. Now the dog will start to feel somewhat more at home in your family, because it will have learned, "I get fed here, I'm treated well here." Now it is time for a rest. First, however, the dog—particularly if it is a puppy—needs to go outdoors again to do its business. In general, follow this rule for the adjustment period: Keep the first few days as calm and structured as possible so that the animal can get accustomed to your daily rhythm and your habits.

Where Should the Dog Sleep?

Every dog needs a place that belongs to it alone, a little spot to which it can withdraw. Make it clear at the outset where the dog is—and is not—allowed to lie.

The daytime sleeping place: It should be in a quiet, draft-free corner and in a room that family members also will be using. Dogs love to lie in a protected spot. A place under a corner table in the kitchen, for example, is ideal. If you want to let your pet have an armchair as its habitual seat, go right ahead. If that is not what you wish, however, you will have to make it off-limits to the dog at the beginning.

A dog is not always happy with the little corner assigned to it—it may seek out its own favorite spot. If its choice is within the given limits, accept the animal's decision and lay a blanket on its place.

The nighttime sleeping place: Whether you let your pet share your bed is a matter of individual taste.

Young dogs chew on hard objects to make it easier for their milk teeth to break through their gums. A special chewing "bone" from the pet store is recommended.

Housebroken in Three Weeks

There is no magic charm that you can use to housebreak your pet quickly and easily. If you follow a few basic rules, however, the puppy will be housebroken within a short time.

The Prerequisite: Take Time

Taking time means this: In the first two to three weeks, do not let your dog out of your sight, around-the-clock. This total involvement will be rewarded, even if it means using some of your vacation. If you fail to

In the backyard, your pet needs a little corner where it can do its business.

invest this time at the outset, weeks or even months may pass before your pet is housebroken. You will achieve this goal swiftly if you keep an eye on the dog at all times and are on hand right away when it needs to do its business.

Take It Out Regularly

After each meal, every time your pet wakes up, and—at the beginning—while you are playing, you will have to take the puppy out. Keep your coat and shoes and the dog's leash handy to save time.

At night, I recommend allowing the pup to sleep near your bed. Choose a small box or a basket that is tall enough to keep the dog from jumping out on its own. Because no dog will soil its own bed, the puppy will whine and try to wake you if it has to go. Then it is time to take it out!

The Tell-tail Sign

If a puppy turns around in a circle and, with its nose to the floor and tail in the air, starts to search, it is an indication that it wants to eliminate. Do not wait until the puppy squats! Drop whatever you are doing and take your pet outside.

The Place for a Puppy's Business

The puppy has to learn right at the start where it is expected to do its business. If you have a backyard, always lead the puppy on its leash to the same spot; do not let it choose its own little corner somewhere or go at random anywhere in the yard. It has to learn to go only to the spot it should continue to use.

In town, it certainly is difficult to find the proper spot in a hurry. Under no circumstances should a dog eliminate in the middle of the sidewalk. This is inconsiderate of others, and in some large cities it now is punishable by a fine. It is ideal if you can find a grassy area, even a small one, nearby. If other dogs already have left their mark there, so much the better. That will encourage the puppy.

Smells can take a puppy's mind off doing its business.

Tip: Even if your puppy's "big business" is still quite small, other people will be grateful to you for removing it. Pet stores sell hygienic, inexpensive supplies for this purpose.

Prompting and Praising

A demand such as "Go on" has the advantage that the dog later on will continue to do its business when it hears this command. Especially on trips, this can be quite useful. Praise the dog at length if everything went well.

If It Happens in the Wrong Place

If the mishap has occurred in your apartment and you are present, a sharp "Phooey!" is sufficient. The "Phooey!" is really useful, however, only if it is spoken immediately after the act. Dogs understand disapproval only if it directly follows the offense. Pushing the dog's nose in the spot, shouting, and whacking the puppy's rear are fundamentally wrong. Don't lose your head; mistakes can happen. Agitation, yelling, and punishment only make the dog unsure and make the road to housebreaking it more difficult. Clean the spot with a disinfectant or a mixture of water and vinegar. Dogs dislike this odor and will avoid the place in the future.

The Newspaper Potty

Especially in an apartment house, it may be tempting to get a young dog used to doing its business on newspapers spread on the apartment floor. I think this is highly unsanitary.

Suddenly No Longer Housebroken?

Once a dog is housebroken, it generally will remain so. As a result of illness or in exceptional situations, however, your pet may suddenly urinate or defecate indoors. Scolding or punishing the animal is quite useless in this situation. Try to determine the cause.

These are some explanations for a dog's suddenly forgetting its training:

- Illness: Take your pet to a veterinarian to find out whether this is the cause.
- Grief: A move, a separation (vacationing without your dog), a change of ownership, a lack of the customary attention, jealousy directed toward a new housemate (a baby, another pet) may unsettle a dog. In such cases, more attention often is helpful.

In the photo:
Do not lose your patience if your pet stops every few yards and sniffs intensely. A dog learns about the world through its nose. Scents contain information vital to the life of a dog.

Extensive sniffing is part of going for a walk.

Does your dog belong in your bed or not? Dog lovers disagree on this subject. Only one thing is certain: If you let a puppy use your bed as a place to sleep, you will have a four-legged friend sharing your bed in the future. No dog understands why it is forbidden as a full-grown animal to do what it was allowed as a puppy.

If the dog is well-groomed and regularly wormed, there certainly are no hygienic concerns. You have to pay attention to only one thing: If you do not want the dog to sleep on your bed, you have to be consistent from the outset. The sweet little puppy that has spent the first few weeks on your bed will continue to demand this right when it is a grown animal. The dog does not understand why it suddenly should relinquish this privilege. If you are of the opinion that a dog has no place in a bed, stay firm in your resolve—even if the little fellow howls the first night. Put its little box or basket near your bed to calm it (see How-To: Housebreaking, page 16).

Even if you do not want to allow the dog in your bed, let it sleep in the bedroom, especially if it is often alone in the daytime. Remember, dogs are pack animals, and the people with whom they live take on the role of the pack. To forbid a dog to seek to be near its humans at night would be, in the animal's eyes, tantamount to exile.

Dogs and Cats

Ideal conditions for the development of a friendship between a cat and a dog are present if the two animals grow up together. If a mature dog is already in the house and a small kitten is added to the household, things generally go well. It is more difficult if a dog is brought into a household where a full-grown cat has domestic rights; cats are headstrong creatures, well known for not letting themselves be forced to do anything. The cat with seniority will be prepared, if need be, to defend its rights against the interloper.

If you want to get a dog and a cat used to each other, take the following suggestions to heart.

The first meeting is especially important; it should not be too stormy, especially on the dog's part. Keep the dog on the leash and lead it carefully toward the cat. As you do so, talk reassuringly to both animals. Subsequently, repeat this sniffing process again and again, watching what develops, and do not leave the animals alone until you are certain that nothing can happen.

Increase familiarity with the other animal's scent by putting in each animal's little basket something that smells of the other—a blanket, for example. In this way, each animal will grow accustomed to the other's smell.

Avoid jealousy. Never neglect the animal with rights of seniority. Pay attention to both animals. For example, two people might sit on the sofa, each holding one of the animals. Pet the animals alternately and talk to them affectionately.

Their friendship pact will be concluded when the cat starts to rub its head against the dog and the dog licks the cat's fur clean.

Dogs and Children

My parents' house was large; it sat at the edge of some woods, at some distance from the other houses. As a little girl, I was always afraid when my parents went out at night. The hall light always had to be burning and the radio playing in the room, and before I went to sleep, I looked under the bed and in the closet to see whether an intruder might be hiding there. One day my father gave me two German shepherds. From that day on, my childhood was transformed. Now, at last, I had no need to be afraid at night, because Alf and Ajax were allowed to sleep next to my bed, and at the age of twelve, I learned some vital things that I had found quite difficult until then: acceptance of responsibility, perseverance, patience, and some measure of punctuality. Whether it rained or snowed, whether I wanted to or not—I walked Alf and Ajax, helped feed them every day at the same time, brushed them, and cleaned their kennel.

My story is certainly no isolated case. Today, dogs are "prescribed" by psychologists, for example, to help the children of divorced parents or children who are ill or handicapped.

The ideal children's dog has to combine many good qualities: It has to be a tireless playmate, a companion who does not take everything the wrong way, is not aggressive, and is neither too sensitive to noise nor too nervous and irritable.

Certain breeds have the reputation of being especially fond of children: boxer, golden retriever, Labrador retriever, schnauzer, Airedale terrier, West Highland white terrier, English sheepdog, beagle, dalmatian, King Charles spaniel, and cocker spaniel.

If you choose a mongrel as your child's companion, find out the characteristics of the dog's parents or ask what character traits are to be expected on the basis of the mixture of breeds.

The age of the child when the dog joins the household is immaterial, because an adult always has to accept responsibility for the dog. The adult should give the child firm guidelines for behavior with the animal. Depending on the child's age, let him or her take on increasing responsibility for the dog's care: buying food, feeding, brushing, walking.

The dog has to learn to respect the child. This is especially important if the dog is a large one. The dog might simply pull the child across the street—with potentially fatal results.

First encounter: Cautiously lead the puppy on its leash toward the cat. Speak encouragingly to both animals.

Basic Rules of Dog Training

Patience, love, and firmness are the foundation of all good training.

1. Begin training as soon as the dog joins your household. In this way, it can learn easily and pleasurably the lessons that an older dog can master only with effort.

2. Get the dog used to fixed commands such as "Phooey, No, Sit, Come."

3. It makes no sense to try to teach the dog too much; teach what it needs to know, and practice until your pet has learned the lesson well.

4. Adjust the difficulty and length of the exercise to the dog's age. Do not overtax your pet.

5. Remember to pet the dog and praise it in a soft voice. An animal that enjoys learning will learn better and faster.

6. If you have to reprimand the animal, do not do so half-heartedly and indecisively; otherwise, your pet will not take you seriously. No lengthy beating around the bush; the dog will not understand it. A concise, sharp expression of disapproval such as "No" or "Phooey" is appropriate.

7. If the reprimand makes no difference, never resort to yelling or hitting—that is the wrong way to treat a dog. A shake administered with the training collar will mean more to your pet, because mother dogs reprimand their puppies by picking them up by the neck and shaking them.

8. Be aware that your dog can indeed connect cause to effect, but only if no time interval separates the two. Do not punish your pet when it returns after a fairly lengthy absence; it will have long forgotten its misdeed. Praise it for coming back; otherwise, the animal will connect its return with the unpleasant experience of scolding and punishment.

9. Remain firm, even though it may be hard at times. Do not allow something today that you forbade the dog to do the previous day. This only confuses the animal.

10. Antiauthoritarian training is totally inappropriate for dogs. Owners who set no clear limits for their dog run the risk of letting the animal set itself up as pack leader. It will no longer take its master seriously and will not obey him.

11. A dog wants to be challenged; otherwise, it will feel its abilities are not being used to capacity and will try to engage your attention with bad behavior.

12. Avoid transmitting your own anxieties to the dog or misusing it for the expression of your human aggressions. Remember, for your dog, you are a role model and a pack leader.

13. Avoid judging the dog from a human point of view. Learning about its way of communicating, its behavior, and its feelings is more important for your life together (see pages 52–59).

A basset hound, nine weeks old— a friendly, but headstrong dog, by no means as indolent as it looks.

Papillons at play: *The self-assured, easily trainable "butterfly dogs" have great vivacity.*

Dog Training, Step by Step

Anyone who brings a dog into the house needs to know that the animal's training begins on the first day. Letting a puppy get away with something because it is still so little is wrong. Even though it may be hard for you to deny the little fellow something, be firm from the outset and show the dog lovingly but definitely what it is and is not allowed to do. The following exercises demonstrate how you can teach your dog what it needs to know to survive and to live with you.

Important: Proceed step by step. Do not ask too much of the dog, and be patient. One dog will learn quickly, whereas another may learn somewhat more slowly.

Lead a young dog this way when you practice "Using the Leash Properly."

Exercise: "Staying Alone"

Every dog has to learn to stay alone; it cannot possibly accompany you everywhere and always. However, as a rule, the dog should not be left alone longer than four hours a day, because such solitude is torture for the animal. Dogs are gregarious by nature. If left too long without anyone to talk to, they waste away and may develop odd patterns of behavior. It is best to start this exercise as soon as your pet is housebroken and you no longer have to watch it constantly.

First step: Take the dog into a room and give the command "Stay." Leave the room and close the door. Now stand quietly outside the door for about five minutes. If the dog scratches at the door and whines, say "No" sharply. Under no circumstances should you go into the room; otherwise, the dog will believe that it brought you back by whining.

If it behaves calmly, you can go in and pet and praise it.

Additional steps: Gradually increase the length of time the dog is left alone. Move farther and farther away from the room, and eventually leave the house.

Exercise: "Using the Leash"

Walking on a leash is one of the fundamental abilities a dog has to acquire, particularly if it lives in a city.

The purpose of the leash is to protect the dog. If an unfamiliar noise startles your pet and it tries to flee in panic, or if it sees a cat and is intent on chasing it, the leash will restrain the dog and keep it from running in front of a car or disappearing forever.

Dogs that hunt have to be leashed in the woods, even if they are able to follow to heel in other situations. Once a dog that likes to hunt has found a scent, the loudest shouts will not hold it back.

During the housebreaking process, you can lead the puppy on its leash to the place where it is allowed to do its business. The leash, then, is not solely for protection; it also is an extension of the dog owner's arm.

Getting Used to the Collar and Leash

Many puppies do not at all like having such a collar placed around their neck. If you notice that your pup is having problems with this when you pick up the dog at the breeder's, do not make it miserable by putting on the collar at once. Instead, put the collar on your pet when you are at home, after it has had a chance to adjust somewhat to the new surroundings. If the puppy completely rejects the collar, try this trick: Put the collar on shortly before you feed the puppy; while it eats, it will be distracted, and afterward perhaps it will not even recall that something had been bothering it. Try a similar trick with the leash. Start with a dry run in your house. Let the dog lead you around a bit, talk to it encouragingly, and praise and pet it.

Using the Leash Properly

To use the leash properly means that you lead the dog, not vice versa. Take the loop of the leash in your right hand, and with your left, hold the leash so that the dog is walking at your left side. Do not hold the leash taut (see drawing, page 22). Now start walking slowly and urge the pup to follow you. Praise it if it follows obediently at your side, and encourage it if it remains hesitantly in its place. Do not lose patience if things are slow at the start. Under no circumstances should you drag the little dog behind you. If it rushes ahead too eagerly, a short tug on the leash is enough of a reprimand. If it strains at its leash, immediately respond with a jerk on the leash; otherwise, your pet will get into a bad habit. After the rebuke, let the leash hang loosely again. The best solution is to use a training collar (see page 11) from the start; it will reinforce the exercise. Never use a choke collar, however. Go through the exercise playfully with the young dog—in the first few weeks, five to ten minutes will be long enough. A yank on the leash is an appropriate form of reprimand for a dog, because mother dogs also grab their naughty pups by the neck and shake them. Yelling, however, is senseless—the dog has excellent hearing. Hitting the animal with a stick or with your hand only upsets it and makes it afraid to approach you when called.

When you walk through town with your dog, keep it on a short leash. The command "Heel" may encourage the dog to walk properly.

My tip: Even if you have a full-grown dog that has never learned to walk correctly on a leash, you can break its habit of straining at the leash. Especially in the case of a large, powerful dog, your yank on the leash has to be vigorous, not too timid.

Patience and love, along with firmness and a great deal of knowledge about the behavior of dogs, are part of the complete training of your pet. Always consider the animal as a partner who needs to be taught a great deal but whom you accept as an independent being.

Looking for a piece of meat...

...shaking pieces of cloth, and

Exercise: "Sit"

If you are to negotiate traffic safely with your dog, it has to learn to sit and wait at the roadside or at the curb before crossing the street. It is understandable that a fidgety puppy has trouble with this kind of exercise. Do not ask too much of your pet; stay patient and remember to pet and praise the dog when it succeeds. As a supportive measure, in this exercise reinforce your loudly spoken command "Sit" by gently pushing the dog down with the palm of your hand just above the animal's rear end (see drawing, page 26).

Exercise: "Coming When Called"

A short time ago, while taking a walk, I witnessed the following scene: A man was standing in a meadow next to some woods and yelling for his Caesar at the top of his lungs. He must have been shouting for quite some time, because he seemed upset, furious, and exhausted.

Suddenly, there was a noise from behind some bushes, and Caesar came racing up. The dog's tongue was hanging all the way out and its coat was wet. The German shepherd obviously had been hunting.

Enraged, the man grabbed his dog and struck its back repeatedly with the leash. Then he put the leash on his pet and, infuriated, dragged the animal after him. The man's reaction is understandable to another human, but what is going on in the dog's mind?

tugging at a ring are all enjoyable games for a dog.

In the photos:
Play with your dog as often as possible. Until they are well advanced in years, most dogs enjoy rollicking games. By offering a paw or nudging you lightly, while assuming the typical "invitation to play" posture, or by bringing you a toy, your pet will indicate that it wants to play with you.

For the animal, the story looks like this: "When I come back, I am punished." Is it worth it, then, to come back? No. Therefore, praise your dog, even if you are furious with it. Otherwise, you are virtually certain to achieve the opposite of what you intend with your punishment. Apart from this, in the case described, the dog should have been on the leash anyway.

Practice coming when called in this way: The puppy, on its own, has such a close tie to its "significant other" that it is not inclined to stray far. Take advantage of this, and call the little fellow from time to time, using its name and the command "Here." If it comes padding up, praise it lavishly and occasionally feed it a dog treat. This reward, however, is to be used sparingly or the dog will always expect to get something if it comes when called.

Exercise: "Off the Leash"

A dog likes nothing better than to be allowed to romp about on its own. If your pet comes when called and has mastered the command "Sit," you have created the prerequisites for permitting it to romp to its heart's content in a park or a field. A dog needs this; its need for exercise and its pace of motion differ greatly from those of the human being who goes walking with it. Caution is in order, however, when walking in the woods or near wooded areas, if your pet is inclined to hunt. It absolutely must be put on a leash.

In city traffic, too, a well-trained dog occasionally can go without a leash, if you are certain that your pet will obey absolutely the commands on which its life depends.

Bad Habits—How to Break Them

Naturally, it is best to make sure from the beginning, through firm training, that no bad habits develop. It is difficult to break a grown dog of bad habits, and your efforts will not always succeed.

It Chews on Everything!

This problem is most common in little puppies. If a grown dog is still going for the furniture or pulling everything to pieces, the owners usually are to blame. A dog that is left alone too much or gets too little attention may protest by becoming destructive. Puppies, however, are like little children; curiosity and playfulness lead them to investigate everything.

The "Sit" exercise: At the beginning, the command "Sit" is reinforced by gently pushing down on the dog's rear with your palm.

While teething, puppies need to chew on hard objects to help the teeth break through the gums. Eventually, their drive to pursue a quarry and to retrieve is awakened, and these instincts also need to be satisfied. The basic principle is this: The more a little dog is kept busy and active, the less it will meddle with things that are not meant for it. With a sharp "Phooey," make it clear to the little pup at the outset what is permitted and what is off limits. You can give your pet appropriate toys (see page 11) to satisfy its need to chew.

Begging at the Table

Let this be said at the beginning: If you never feed your dog at the table, you will never have this problem. Unfortunately, however, the intelligent dog quickly locates the weak spot in the family and concentrates determinedly on this person. Usually, the dog emerges the victor. Here are some basic rules and tips to make it easier for you:

1. Divide the dog's daily ration of food, and feed your pet twice a day. This will make it less inclined to beg.

2. Give the dog its food while you are eating your own meal so that the animal has the feeling of eating along with the rest of its "pack."

3. Stay firm: Do not give in to your pet's melancholy gaze or pawing.

4. If a reprimand does not keep the dog from bringing its nose closer and closer to your plate, hold a sliced onion or piece of lemon under its nose. Dogs dislike these smells, and in the future—if you repeat your response often enough—your pet will associate begging at the table with this unpleasant experience.

5. If your pet is an especially persistent beggar—perhaps already spoiled by a previous owner—or if you cannot maintain your resolve, then live with the situation, or feed the dog before you eat and lock it in an adjoining room while you enjoy your meal.

Jumping on People

Boisterously jumping up on pet owners and their visitors, frequently in combination with a wet "kiss," is part of puppies' way of communicating. This gesture of welcome is innate in dogs. Young dogs greet their mother in this way and beg for food.

Some dog owners do not mind if their clothes are continually covered with dirty paw prints; they calmly accept this as proof of their pet's affection. Unfortunately, these dog lovers forget that other people may not agree with them. After all, this kind of tempestuous greeting can do more than soil clothing; ladies' stockings develop runs, and a heavy Saint Bernard easily can knock a grown man to the ground. Break this bad habit while your puppy is young; otherwise, you will continue to annoy other people with your ill-trained dog. This is the best way:

Step 1: Fend off the dog and order it to stop: With a young dog: Hold up your palm and reprimand the dog with a chiding "Phooey" or "No."

With an older, larger dog that already has formed this bad habit and no longer responds to a simple reprimand: If the dog leaps toward you, draw up your knee so that the dog strikes it. Seize the animal by its front paws and throw it back. In addition, reprimand it by saying "No" or "Phooey."

Step 2: Preserve the dog's eagerness to welcome you: Your pet wants to display its pleasure at your returning home and intends nothing

bad by its tempestuous manner of welcome. If it meets exclusively with resistance, it will be irritated. Do not deprive your dog of its pleasure in greeting you; instead, offer it a substitute form of greeting that is acceptable to you. For example:

• Use a training procedure: If the dog wants to jump up on you, give the command "Sit." Then praise and pet the animal to your heart's content. You might also ask it to give you its paw.

• Divert the drive to be active: Roll a ball on the floor and play with the dog. Go into the kitchen with your pet and offer it a small reward.

Important: If other people permit the dog to jump up, all your effort will have been in vain.

Playing with Your Dog

In the wolf pack, it is the father's job to train the growing pups to become orderly members of the pack. Untiringly, he romps with them and teaches them, through these games, the lessons they need for life. In the dog-human relationship, it is important that dogs learn to cuddle and play with their humans.

In playing with your dog, always retain the role of respected pack leader. Do not allow the dog to bite your heels or defend its prey against you by growling and snapping. If you fail to set limits, the dog will cease to take you seriously, and soon it will pose as pack leader itself. In my experience, almost all dogs enjoy the following games.

Hide-and-seek: When the dog is not paying attention, quickly hide behind a door or sofa or, if in the yard, behind a hedge or in some bushes. Now call and beckon your pet—and the dog will come running in a jiffy,

Praise, not punishment, is the most important foundation for successful dog training. A dog should cooperate happily in its training, not follow commands out of fear.

27

This seven-week-old puppy looks hungrily at the slice of meat.

In the photo:
If small children are growing up together with a dog, do not neglect proper hygiene, but do not be overly anxious. It is important that the dog be wormed regularly.

beside itself with joy once it has found you.

Chasing and retrieving a quarry: Tie something interesting to a long rope—perhaps a piece of hide, a small broom, or a box containing something that will rattle. Now run out ahead; your pet will be right behind you. To keep the game from growing boring, let the dog get the quarry now and then—it will carry it away proudly.

Tracing a scent: Show the dog a piece of meat or sausage, then hide it in a box or behind a rock.

If the dog is young, let it watch while you hide the meat. An older dog should sit and wait until you come

back. If the young dog has problems, give it some help in finding the scent.

Extensive praise will increase your pet's enjoyment of the quest.

Tugging and shaking: A linen rag or a piece of leather, knotted several times, can be seized by your dog and shaken thoroughly. Pull on one end from time to time, and eventually let the dog run away with its quarry. If it brings the rag back, praise it and pet it—and start the game over, if you wish.

Throwing balls and sticks: Chasing after balls and sticks is always enjoyable for dogs, even quite old ones. The experience of veterinari-

Dalmatians—the puppy (eight weeks old) is inviting its mother to play.

ans, however, proves that it is precisely the beloved stick that often causes the worst injuries: If the stick is too long, it can injure the dog's mouth when the animal bites down eagerly. The golden rule of stick throwing: Look for a short stick with blunt ends, no longer than half the dog's height at shoulder level.

Important: Remove sharp little pieces of twigs from the stick, because they can injure the dog's gums.

In the photo:
Dalmatians are bright, adaptable dogs that are easy to train. These tireless runners are suitable only for athletically inclined owners who enjoy running, bicycling, or horseback riding.

Out and About with Your Dog

Modern dogs are highly mobile animals. Riding in cars and elevators, traveling by airplane, or running alongside a bicycle—they participate in all the modes of locomotion used by their owners. What they most enjoy continues to be the daily walk.

How to Enjoy Taking a Walk

The availability of a yard, however large it may be, does not relieve you of the responsibility of taking your pet for a daily walk. The walk not only provides your dog with exercise and an opportunity to do its business, it also adds some variety to the animal's life and is a source of new impressions. A walk also will do you good; this daily stroll with your dog costs nothing and will result in increased fitness on your part. Long-term studies conducted in the United States prove that it is not a high-paced competitive sport, but regular, brisk walking, that leads to a longer life. Console yourself with this thought when you do not feel like walking the dog!

The Length of the Walk

It depends on the age, overall constitution, and breed of your dog. The pug and the Pekinese, for example, tend to be leisurely strollers, quite happy with going out for a half hour three times a day.

Breeds that like to run, such as the Irish setter, the dalmatian, or the larger mongrels, need two to three hours of exercise per day.

Every healthy dog needs to take walks and play with its owner as often as possible. Spending hours alone or being separated from you for weeks can so disturb your pet's peace of mind that it forgets its training and suddenly does its business indoors.

Sniffing and Marking

A walk is not merely a chance for the dog to get exercise; it also gives the animal sufficient scope to fulfill its needs.

Sniffing: The dog wants to sniff wherever members of the same species have left their calling cards or wherever there is some other intriguing smell. Do not keep pulling your pet away if it stops and wants to smell a spot thoroughly.

Marking is a basic need of every male dog. Do not be surprised if your pet lifts its leg ten times or more during a walk. This is the way it marks its territory and puts its own personal scent on top of its predecessor's.

Contact with Other Dogs

It is important, especially for a growing dog, to be together with other members of its species, so that it can learn to associate with them in a natural, uninhibited way.

Take your pet as frequently as possible to places where you will encounter other dog owners with their four-legged friends. Communication with other dogs, free play, romping, and playful struggles to establish hierarchy will socialize your pet.

You need to know what happens when dogs get together. Male dogs, particularly younger ones, tend to mount each other when they play. Do not recoil in horror and begin to moralize. Your dog is not abnormal.

This effort to dominate one another is part of the game, a component of establishing a hierarchy.

- If a big, strange dog approaches, do not make the mistake of pulling your dog away at once. By doing so, you merely will transmit your own anxiety to your pet and make the dog into a coward. Subsequently, it will try to flee at every approach, yowl hysterically, or snap right away in fear, biting the other animal without cause.

- If you immediately pick up your dog when another one approaches, you are not doing it a favor either; you are giving your pet a sense of superiority. If the little animal, from its perch on high, then starts to bark impudently, a dog that outranks yours in the animals' hierarchy will not stand for this behavior; it will punish your dog immediately or at the next opportunity.

- Unfortunately, we now encounter disturbed dogs with increasing frequency. Misguided training and improper care have eliminated, to a dangerous degree, these animals' inhibitions about biting. Only one thing will help here: If possible, avoid the dog; if a mishap cannot be prevented and the dog does bite your pet, report the animal's owner at once. A muzzle could be the answer! This is the only way to protect people and other dogs from these dangerous animals.

In the Woods or at the Edge of the Woods

In such places, a dog needs to be leashed, especially if it has any inclination to hunt. Even if you let a well-trained non-hunting dog off its leash, it always should stay near you.

Dogs That Are Crazy About Water

If you do not restrain them in time, nothing can keep these dogs from plunging into cool water, summer or winter. If your pet is crazy about water, put swimming trips on your agenda. Train your dog to enter the water only with your permission. Unsupervised swimming can be dangerous for a dog. Rivers, canals, and dams with concrete banks can become death traps for dogs. Their paws slip on the smooth, high concrete edges, and once the balls of their feet are injured, they cannot get back to shore again without help. There is also a danger that a dog will catch cold. When a dog is hot after romping and racing about, it should not jump immediately into the water. Short-haired dogs (like boxers), in particular, have a tendency to develop colds in these circumstances.

Tip: For many dogs—golden retrievers, for example—swimming, playing in the water, and romping are innate, basic needs. One of the purposes for which these dogs have been bred is to retrieve game (ducks, for example) from the water. Consequently, they have to fulfill these needs—to retrieve and to be in the water, often—or they will feel deprived of incentive.

A solid rubber ring is a favorite dog toy that you can take along on every walk.

E nglish sheep-
dogs dearly
love to play; they
are fond of children,
good-natured, lively,
adaptable, and also
self-assured and
independent—in
short, lovable family
pets. Suitable for
owners who have a
great deal of room,
enjoy outings with
their pet, and have
sufficient patience
to comb this dog's
long, thick coat for
about 20 minutes
a day.

If Your Dog Runs Away

Sometimes all your caution is of no avail; a rabbit speeds past, or a male dog gets the scent of a female in heat —and your pet is gone. What now?

Stay patient and calm: Stay at the spot where the dog ran away. Call it from time to time, and wait. There is a great chance that your pet will return after its excursion. If it does, praise it. It is senseless to thrash it (see Exercise: "Coming When Called," page 24).

Call the police and animal protection organizations: Your dog always should wear its tag or capsule with your name and telephone number (page 11). With this information, it will be easy to identify your pet if it ends up at the ASPCA or at a police station. If the dog is tattooed (page 14), your chances of getting it back are even greater. Call the nearest animal hospital or the veterinarians in your neighborhood; your pet may have been in an accident, and someone may have taken it to a doctor.

This type of wire screen for a car window is easily installed. It lets the dog get fresh air when it has to wait in the car.

Taking a Bike Ride

Not every dog is suited to run alongside your bicycle. Short-legged dogs enjoy bike trips most when sitting in a little basket attached to the handlebars, and slow, heavy dogs like Saint Bernards are totally unsuited for bike rides. If your dog is a runner, keep this in mind: Do not start training your pet until it is one year old. Adjust your pace to that of your dog.

Important: If you train your pet daily to run beside your bike, there will be consequences; just as in the case of a top athlete, the dog's training should not be ended abruptly. Ease off gradually.

Riding in a Car

For most dogs, riding in a car now is just as routine as the daily walk. Many dogs are crazy about cars; as soon as the door is opened, they jump in and take their place.

From the outset, a dog needs to have its own permanent place in the car. A small dog should be in front, on the floor mat in front of the passenger seat, and a large animal belongs on the back seat or in the cargo space of a station wagon. Protective screens or dog nets, available in pet stores, keep the dog from climbing to the front or flying through the car if you brake suddenly.

During the trip, put an antiskid mat or blanket under your pet.

On longer trips, be sure to take regular breaks so that the dog can get some exercise, do its business, and drink fresh water. In summer, when temperatures are high, leave the animal alone in the car only in case of emergency—and then only for a few minutes. Every year, dogs die in cars in which the internal temperature has climbed too high. Always leave a window open so the dog can get enough air. You can purchase window screens that are easily installed (drawing, left).

Using Public Transportation

Traveling by train or using other public means of transportation usually is not a problem, if your dog is well trained. Most railroads, however, require that your dog must travel in a container in the baggage car. With airlines, too, it is essential to verify the arrangements before you purchase tickets. You will need to consider pressurized luggage compartments and the appropriate size container for your dog. Some airlines lend containers;

others rent them; a safe bet is to purchase your own. In short, get the necessary information before you set out on your trip. Remember, your dog also requires a ticket.

Vacationing with Your Dog

Every year, thousands of dogs are put out and abandoned, most of them during the peak vacation period. My work with animal advocacy organizations has made me familiar with this sad fact, but I am unable to reconstruct or to comprehend the chain of thought that leads to such acts.

Take your dog along on vacation. If you organize things properly, a vacation with your pet will be a fine experience for the entire family.

It is impossible to vacation with your dog in, for example, England, Ireland, Sweden, Norway, and Finland, because these countries require a quarantine period of several months.

The dog needs papers, because almost all countries demand proof of rabies vaccination upon entry. In many countries, an official certificate of health issued by a veterinarian is also required. Ask your veterinarian what the regulations are. If in doubt, contact the appropriate consulate.

When on vacation in hot countries or, for example, in the South, your dog also will need a shady spot. After swimming in salt water, give your pet a shower or spray it with a hose.

Hotels, pensions, and camping grounds where dogs are welcome are plentiful. Travel agencies, pet stores, and bookstores can supply you with brochures and books that contain addresses of accommodations that accept dogs, as well as locations of "dog beaches." For more information, contact: Gaines TWT, P.O. Box 8172,

Kankakee, Illinois 60901, and ask for "Touring with Towser," a directory of hotels and motels that accommodate guests with dogs.

If Your Dog Is Staying Home While You Travel

Not all countries and vacation spots are suitable for dog owners and pets interested in a joint vacation. For instance, it is better to leave your dog at home than to subject it to a two-week stay in New York City! An ideal solution is to leave the animal in the care of friends or relatives who know it well.

Ask your dog's breeder also; he may have room. To board your dog in a kennel, you will have to reserve a place early, and you also should inspect the facilities ahead of time. Ask the American Boarding Kennel Association, 4575 Galley Road, Suite 400A, Colorado Springs, Colorado 80915, or your veterinarian to give you the names of reliable boarding kennels.

This sturdy, easy-to-clean carrier is practical if you have to transport a sick dog to the veterinarian or if you wish to take your pet along on airplane trips.

Proper Nutrition

Appropriate Food

You are not doing your dog a favor if you look at its nutritional requirements with human eyes. There is a considerable difference between the ways humans and dogs eat. The very fact that food spends much less time in a dog's gastrointestinal tract than in a human's indicates that the dog's food has to be many times more concentrated than the food you eat. To feed your pet leftovers, therefore, would not be healthy for it. It is true that over the many centuries of domestication, dogs have changed their eating habits, but in terms of their nutrition, they have remained wolves in many respects.

Ancestor Wolf and Its Diet

Wolves—and hence dogs—fall into the category of carnivorous, or meat-eating, animals. This concept always creates misunderstandings, because the wolf does not eat meat exclusively. As a beast of prey, it lives chiefly on small animals; it hunts rabbits, hares, and—when hunting in a pack—deer. Its quarries are herbivores, or plant eaters, in whose stomachs and entrails is found predigested plant pulp, which the dog also consumes. In addition, it eats varying quantities of fresh plant matter (fruits, grasses, roots, herbs).

Naturally, you cannot serve your dog its prey at mealtime or send it out to hunt for the noon meal. You can, however, feed it what it needs—pro-

A Yorkshire terrier, twelve weeks old—an ideal dog for small apartments. It requires training just as firm as that of a large dog.

teins, fats, carbohydrates, vitamins, minerals, and raw fiber. Whether you use commercially prepared food or fix your pet's meals yourself is unimportant.

Commercial Dog Food

There is much to be said for the use of commercial dog foods. They are quick and convenient to prepare and easy to store, and they contain everything the animal requires. Dog food is commercially available in various forms. It can be purchased in pet stores, which also sell special food for puppies.

Moist Food

About 75 percent of this food is water. Sold in cans, it is a very common type of dog food. Some variety in your pet's diet can be achieved by using different brands and kinds of foods (chicken, game, beef).

Feeding tip: With some products, the daily portions recommended are too generous. Keep an eye on your dog. If it is getting too fat, give it less food and make sure it is getting enough exercise. Preferably, use canned food with few chemical additives. If your pet's teeth and gums are to stay healthy, it needs something hard to bite in addition to soft canned food (see Foods to gnaw, page 38).

My tip: I have had good experience with ready-made dog meals that are based on fresh meat. They contain no preservatives, dyes, or other additives to make the product attractive.

Golden retrievers are passionate swimmers; even in winter, they are not afraid to go in the water.

Semimoist and Dry Foods

Concentrated, high-energy nutritious food, with a water content of 25 to 30 percent.

Important: Make sure your dog drinks enough water. The moisture removed from the food has to be replaced. Before giving dry food to your pet, you can soften it in broth prepared with vegetables or bones or in water.

Kibbled Foods

Kibbles, or meals, contain mineral substances and vitamins. If you feed your pet only canned food (see Moist Food, page 36), kibbled dog food may enrich its diet. If you give it fresh meat (page 40) or canned meat, add kibble in this ratio: $1/3$ dog kibble to $2/3$ meat. Kibbled foods are not suitable as your pet's sole diet.

Poor, fat dog—overweight leads to health problems.

Treats

Vitamin drops, dog chocolate, crackers—there are a thousand little snacks available to surprise or reward your pet. However tempting the array of products offered, do not make a practice of feeding your dog between meals.

Foods to gnaw: Dog biscuits, air-dried strips of cow's rumen or cowhide, cows' hooves, buffalo hide bones, veal cartilage (especially for small dogs), or beef knuckle bones. Offer a choice once or twice a week.

Important information about bones: Knuckle bones should come from cattle or calves. Do not use small beef bones, chicken, turkey, pork, or lamb bones; they will splinter into pieces with sharp points and injure your dog's stomach and intestines. These injuries can prove fatal.

Food Amounts

If you use commercially prepared food, you generally can use the manufacturer's recommendations as a guideline. If you prepare your pet's food yourself, calculate the amounts carefully (page 39). Dogs' caloric requirements vary greatly from one

Food dishes that can be raised and lowered are quite convenient for larger dogs, such as boxers or Airedale terriers.

animal to the next and also depend on the amount of exercise the dog gets. For this reason, keep checking to see whether your pet is eating too much or too little. If you can feel the dog's ribs, fine. If they stand out too much—so that they are visible in a short-haired dog—the animal is too thin. If you have to probe for them with your fingertips or if you no longer can feel them at all, the dog is too fat.

An overweight dog can be helped by a diet. Ask your veterinarian.

Drinking

Fresh water ought to be on hand at all times, and it should be replaced every day. If the weather is quite hot or if the dog has eaten dry food, it will need more liquid.

Milk, strictly speaking, counts as a supplementary food. Only very young dogs should be given cow's milk or puppy milk products. The intestines of a grown dog may react poorly to fresh milk (as they lack the enzyme required to digest and assimilate milk sugar), and diarrhea can result, particularly if you feed your pet milk and meat at the same meal. Offer milk only if your dog likes it and can tolerate it. Most dogs, however, accept fresh goat's milk and tolerate milk products, such as cottage cheese, yogurt, or buttermilk.

What Does a Young Dog Eat?

Either give your pet the special puppy chow available in pet stores, or try the following: about 3 ounces (90 g) of medium-boiled egg, 13 ounces (360 g) of pot cheese (farmer cheese) or cottage cheese, 2 tablespoons of cooking oil, 2 tablespoons of bran, 13 ounces (360 g) of beef, 3/4 ounce (20 g) of liver—both meats cooked and cut into small pieces—and a vitamin preparation, about 1 ounce (32 g) for every 2 pounds (1 kg) of body weight. You can feed this to your puppy until it is about one year old. This daily ration is intended for a dog that will weigh about 22 pounds (10 kg) when fully grown.

Feeding Times and Places

A dog should always be fed at the same time. After eating, it needs to rest. Large dogs, in particular, ought not to be walked right after eating (a twisted stomach may result). Feeding times:

- after the second month, four times a day;
- after the fourth month, three times a day;
- after the sixth month, twice a day.
- A grown dog may be fed once a day, preferably at midday, but the amount may be divided into two meals.

I find the latter method preferable, because a dog that is fed twice a day is less apt to beg and to gulp its food.

Feeding place: Do not disturb your pet while it is eating. Put its dish in a quiet corner, preferably in the kitchen, where the floor can be washed.

Important Feeding Rules

- Observe regular mealtimes; the dog's stomach will get accustomed to this.
- After eating, the full, contented animal should be allowed to rest. Postpone the walk to a later time or go before mealtime.
- Throw away any leftover food.
- Always serve your pet's food at room temperature.
- Leftovers from your table are not suitable food for your dog; potatoes, noodles, gravy, and cake are not appropriate dog foods.

This highly suitable dish made of steel has an antiskid rubber rim on the bottom.

Basic Plan for Home-Cooked Meals				
Size of Dog	Meat	Fats	Cereals	Dairy Products
Larger dogs (such as German shephard, Airedale terrier)	10 –14 oz (300 –400 g)	1–1³/₄ oz (30 –50 g) (= 2 T oil)	5¹/₃ –7 oz (150 –200 g)	2 T
Medium-sized and small dogs (such fox terrier, cocker spaniel, dachshund)	5¹/₃ –7 oz (150 –200 g)	³/₄ –1 oz (20 –30 g) (= 1 T oil)	2¹/₂ –3¹/₂ oz (70 –100 g)	1 T
Minature or toy dogs	3 –3¹/₂ oz (80 –100 g)	¹/₃ –¹/₂ oz (10 –15 g) (= 1 tsp oil)	1–1³/₄ oz (30 –50 g)	1–2 tsp

Important: Enrich every daily serving with a mixture of vitamins and minerals (see Important Supplements, page 41).

You invite people you like to lovingly prepared meals. Why not cook for your beloved pets on occasion? A home-cooked meal will add some variety to a dog's diet. It is important that the food contain all the major nutritional groups.

Comments on the Basic Plan for Meals

On page 39, you will find the basic plan for preparing home-cooked meals for dogs. It specifies the amounts of the ingredients described on these two How-To pages. Using this plan as a basis, you can prepare meals with a variety of tastes for your pet.

The ingredients: The "building blocks" of the meal (meat, fats, cereals, dairy products, supplements) are given. Include all of these elements in your preparations, but feel free to vary the ingredients themselves. For example, use chicken instead of beef.

Remember: The supplements are important (see page 41).

The statements of quantity: The amount given is for one day's ration for a healthy, full-grown dog with a normal opportunity for exercise (walks).

Show dogs and nursing mother dogs have to be fed differently; ask your veterinarian for advice.

Dog size: Some guidelines:
• Larger dogs—all dogs taller than about 24 inches (62 cm) at shoulder level, with the exception of extremely large dogs such, as Great Danes or Saint Bernards.
• Medium-sized and small dogs—all dogs between 10 inches (24 cm) and 24 inches (62 cm) tall at shoulder level.
• Miniature or toy dogs—all dogs less than 10 inches (24 cm) high at shoulder level.

Ingredients and Their Preparation

A nourishing, home-cooked meal for a dog entails a bit of work, but if your pet enjoys it, it is worth the trouble. The ingredients listed below should be used in the amounts specified.

Important: Use only the best ingredients. Spoiled food, such as a table scrap, has no place in a dog's dish.

Bones made of raw hide can be gnawed by all dogs.

Meat

Always use cooked meat, cut in small pieces. These meats are suitable: lean muscle cuts of beef, veal, horse meat, or chicken. For variety, try these: tripe, heart, liver, and kidneys, no more than once a week. If these foods cause your dog to have diarrhea, discontinue their use.

My tip: Poultry and deboned fish—both cooked—are ideal as a bland diet for dogs with gastrointestinal complaints and for dogs that need to lose weight. Amounts: same as for meat.

Fats

If fats are not available in the form of meat fat (fatty meat), use vegetable oil or butter in the amounts given.

Cereal Products

These are suitable if cooked: whole-grain rice, cereal flakes (oatmeal or wheat flakes), millet or barley gruel (crush millet and barley before cooking). These may be eaten uncooked: four-grain flake mixture (baby food, for example) or dog kibble (use instant types in both instances).

Important: If you use kibble, follow these rules:
• $2/3$ meat, $1/3$ kibble.
• If the kibbled food contains added vitamins (see package), do not use vitamin and mineral supplements.

Dairy Products

These are suitable: cottage cheese or pot cheese (farmer cheese).

These puppies, six weeks old, are thoroughly enjoying their first solid food.

Important Supplements

Remember: Every meal has to be enriched with one of the supplements listed below.

Exception: Supplements are not necessary if dog kibble with added vitamins is used.

Option 1: Use one of the mixtures of vitamins and minerals sold in pet stores, as directed by the instructions on the package.

Option 2: Use the following homemade mixture (containing all the required substances):
- Brewer's yeast flakes: Larger dogs, 1 tablespoon; all others, 1 teaspoon.
- Boiled egg: Larger dogs, 1 egg; all others, 1/2 egg.

- Bonemeal: Larger dogs, about 3/4 ounce (20 g); medium-sized and small dogs, about 1/3 ounce (10 g); miniature dogs, about 1/5 ounce (5 g).
- Raw and chopped in a blender: 1/2 apple, 1/2 carrot, 1 lettuce leaf, some parsley. Reduce amounts slightly for small dogs.
- Mix all ingredients well.

Preparation

Let the cooked foods come to room temperature. Mix all the ingredients of the dog's meal thoroughly. Make sure the dog is not picking and choosing. If your pet is picking out only the pieces of meat, briefly mix the entire meal in a blender. Some dogs, however, will refuse to eat the meal afterward.

Supplementary Food to Nibble

Once or twice a week (take your choice; see page 38).

Taking Care of Your Dog

The care you bestow on your pet is part of the affection you show the dog. You ensure that the animal feels comfortable, that its ears, eyes, and teeth are clean, and that it is free of vermin.

Coat Care

If coat care is performed correctly, your pet will enjoy this essential part of its grooming.

Important: Start by getting the young dog accustomed to regular grooming of its coat, performed in a spirit of play and, above all, with patience at all times.

Short-haired dogs (for example, boxers, pinschers, and short-haired dachshunds): Brush your pet's entire body once a week, more frequently when it is shedding. After brushing, rub the animal's coat with a chamois skin to make it shiny.

Thick-haired (such as German shepherds) and **long-haired dogs** (such as Maltese, collies, and English sheepdogs): First, carefully comb out the coat with a large-toothed metal comb. If the fur is long and silky (Shih Tzu), comb it again with a fine-toothed comb. Finally, brush the coat with a long-bristled brush. If the coat of hair is very thick (English sheepdog), try a sturdy wire brush or a curry comb with curved wire teeth.

Important: Never pull on the hair; carefully untangle any knots with your fingers. Use scissors to cut off any heavily matted knots, being careful not to cut the dog's skin. Large matted portions should be removed at a dog grooming salon or by a veterinarian.

Additional hair care in a grooming salon: Curly-haired dogs (poodle) have to be clipped two or three times a year. Wire-haired and rough-haired breeds (Airedale terrier, fox terrier, wire-haired dachshund, schnauzer) need to be trimmed every four months. In this procedure, dead hair is plucked out by hand and removed with a stripping knife, while the remaining hair is styled. As a dog novice, you should leave cutting and trimming to the professionals in the grooming salon.

Tools for grooming your pet's coat (top to bottom): A two-sided brush, a large-toothed comb, and a brush with natural bristles.

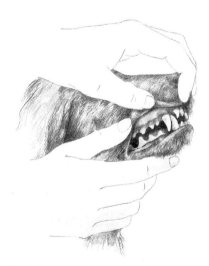

Look into your dog's mouth once a month. If tartar has formed or a tooth is damaged, take your pet to the veterinarian.

When a Bath Is Necessary

Whenever your pet is smelly and dirty, follow these rules for bathing a dog:
- Use a shampoo formulated for dogs.
- Place an antiskid mat in the basin or tub.
- Use a hand-held spray attachment with care. Wet the dog's head last, and while doing so, cover its ears and eyes with your hand to shield them.
- After the bath, rub your pet dry with a towel, comb its coat, and either blow-dry its fur (recommended for Yorkshires) or let it dry in a well-heated room.

Eye Care

Particularly for breeds with "pop eyes," such as the Chihuahua, and dogs with drooping eyelids, such as the basset hound, it is necessary to remove eye secretions daily. Using a soft, unscented paper tissue, carefully wipe the corners of the eyes. You can moisten the tissue with eyebright, available in pharmacies. This old natural remedy will soothe irritated eyes and dissolve encrusted lacrimal fluid.

Ear Care

Look in your dog's ears from time to time; if too much earwax is visible, cleaning is necessary. Take a soft paper tissue, put a few drops of baby oil on it, and wipe out the ear. Cleaning with cotton swabs is inadvisable because of the danger of injury.

Go to your veterinarian if you notice any of the following:
- a blackish-brown, relatively dry discharge in the ear (ear mites);
- excessive earwax;
- the skin is reddened and hot; or
- the dog is constantly shaking its head and scratching its ear (inflammation or foreign body in the ear).

Regular ear care is important. Put a few drops of baby oil on a soft paper towel and carefully wipe out your pet's ears.

Checking the Teeth

Look in your pet's mouth at least once a month. If you see tartar there, have a veterinarian remove it.

You also will have to take your pet to a veterinarian in these cases:
- if your dog has bad breath;
- if a tooth is broken or if the gums are inflamed; or
- if there is an excessive flow of saliva, particularly if it is mixed with blood.

Nail Care

It is best to have the veterinarian examine your pet's nails during the routine checkup or when the animal is being vaccinated. Trimming a dog's nails demands experience. The danger of injury is great, and a layman is wise not to meddle with the nails.

Removing Ticks and Fleas

Every dog owner has to get used to the idea that his pet occasionally will play host to ticks and fleas.

Ticks are especially common in early summer. You can expect your dog to bring back several from every walk. Even if you immediately search the dog's coat for these minute blood-suckers, you usually will not find them until they have increased in size.

Remove ticks in the following way:
- Saturate a cotton pad with alcohol or cooking oil.
- Cover the tick with the pad for several minutes.
- Working counterclockwise, rotate the tick with two fingers, tweezers, or tick nippers (sold in pet stores), and draw it out. Make sure the tick's head is not left embedded in the dog's skin; otherwise, the spot will become infected.

Important: The carriers (vectors) of the *Borrelia burgdorferi* bacterium that causes Lyme disease are *Ixodes* ticks. Hosts—animals that the ticks feed on—include migratory birds, deer, skunks, rabbits, mice, raccoons, cattle, horses, cats, and humans. Lyme disease—a joint disease (arthritis), often accompanied by fever, lethargy, and loss of appetite—is believed to be transmittable from animals to man.

Fleas: Your dog can get fleas at any time of year. If you discover a flea or flea excrement—tiny dark flecks that leave red spots on damp paper or a white cloth—try the following:
- Bathe the dog with a special shampoo or cover its entire body with powder.
- Wash the blankets on which your pet sleeps, and powder its basket and nearby areas of carpet.
- The treatment will succeed only if repeated at least three times at one-week intervals.

A German shepherd, nine weeks old—an intelligent, brave dog that needs a great deal of exercise and good training.

- Preparations for use in combatting fleas are available in pet stores and drugstores.

Important: Fleas not only are pesky, but they also serve as intermediate hosts for tapeworms, which your dog can get by eating a flea. In the event of a flea infestation, treat your dog for worms as well.

Flea and Tick Collar

As a preventive measure, have your pet wear a collar that will help combat fleas and ticks (available in pet stores). I recommend, however, that the collar be worn only when the dog is outdoors, that is, when taking its walk or spending time in the yard. This is advisable because the preparation with which the collar is coated will rub off onto the dog's hair and be ingested when the animal cleans its fur. Pet stores also offer a so-called organic collar containing essential oils; it also is said to be helpful.

I advise against the use of the tablets and tinctures recommended by many veterinarians. They introduce into the dog's bloodstream toxic substances that will kill the bloodsuckers. One hesitates to imagine how the dog's liver and other organs are burdened by this constant poisoning.

An Afghan hound, fifteen months old. This beautiful breed of sight hound is not easy to train.

Prevention and Diseases

A dog cannot tell you where it hurts. Consequently, watching your pet and noting changes in its behavior and appearance are part and parcel of the duties required of the person who has assumed responsibility for the animal. Almost all diseases are accompanied by apathy—listlessness, failure to enjoy playing or taking a walk—and loss of appetite. The table on pages 50 and 51 shows how to interpret additional behavioral signs and what diseases they may indicate. Do not postpone the trip to the veterinarian too long; it is better to take your dog once too often than too seldom.

Important: The worming treatments and vaccinations listed on page 47 are indispensable preventive measures.

What You as a Dog Owner Should Do

The veterinarian has to rely on your cooperation, not only in describing your pet's symptoms, but also in administering medicines and taking the dog's temperature.

Report Your Observations

The better you can describe what you have noticed about your dog's behavior, the more easily and accurately the veterinarian can make a diagnosis. These questions are important:

- When and what did the dog last eat?
- What is the animal's feces like? Watery or too firm? Are its bowels not moving at all? What color are the stools? Light? Black? Do they have an unpleasant odor? Are the bowel movements bloody?
- Has the dog vomited? Is it bringing up phlegm?
- Have you noticed anything else that seems abnormal?

Taking the Dog's Temperature

The dog's normal temperature ranges from 100 to 102°F (38–39°C). Higher or lower temperatures (above or below normal) may be a symptom of illness.

When taking your pet's temperature, raise the dog's tail and keep a firm hold on it.

This is the correct procedure (drawing, page 46):

- Use a thermometer that will give a reading quickly—a nonbreakable thermometer for measuring children's temperature, with a digital display. Use this thermometer exclusively for the dog!
- Lubricate the tip with some petroleum jelly or cooking oil.
- Have a second person help you by holding the dog's head firmly in the crook of his arm and talking soothingly to the animal.
- Lift up the dog's tail and insert the thermometer about 3/4 inch (2 cm) into the anus.
- Holding the dog still, leave the thermometer in place for about 60 seconds. Digital thermometers that signal the completion of the measurement by emitting a beeping sound are quite practical.

Giving Medicine

A well-trained dog should let its mouth be opened at any time. Hold the animal's upper jaw with one hand, and gently press down on the lower jaw. If the dog clenches its teeth, lightly press its chops against its teeth.

- It is best to roll up tablets in small strips of meat. If this does not work, place the tablet as far back as possible on the dog's tongue, hold its mouth closed, and check to see whether the animal may have succeeded in spitting the tablet out again. With flat-faced dogs (Pekinese, pug), make sure you do not hold the nostrils shut.
- If you have to administer medicine in liquid form, have the veterinarian give you a disposable syringe (without a needle, of course). Draw the liquid up into the syringe and squirt it into the dog's mouth at the side.

Important Preventive Measures

Never dispense with worming and vaccinations; they are the most important measures you can take to keep your pet healthy.

Worming

Worm treatments are necessary to keep your dog healthy.

Worm your pet at these ages:
- four weeks,
- six weeks,
- eight weeks (followed by first vaccination),
- twelve weeks (followed by second vaccination),
- six months,
- nine months,

then twice a year. Plan each treatment so that it immediately precedes a vaccination (see Immunization schedule, right), because the dog has to be healthy when it is inoculated.

Immunization Schedule

To protect your pet from fatal diseases, you have to arrange for it to be vaccinated. The inoculations are recorded on the vaccination certificate you receive when you buy the dog.

Important: The dog has to be wormed before every vaccination (see Worming, left).

A puppy is vaccinated at these ages:
- eight to nine weeks against distemper, hepatitis, leptospirosis, parvoviral gastroenteritis, and rabies;
- twelve to fourteen weeks against distemper, hepatitis, leptospirosis, parvoviral gastroenteritis, and rabies.

Every year thereafter, in alternation, a mature dog is given these inoculations:
- First year: combination of three injections against leptospirosis, parvoviral gastroenteritis, and rabies. (The shot for distemper and hepatitis is good for two years.)
- Second year: combination of five injections against distemper, hepatitis, leptospirosis, parvoviral gastroenteritis, and rabies.
- Third year: combination of three.
- Fourth year: combination of five, and so forth.

Health Traps for Dogs

Aside from the dangerous diseases of dogs—against which your pet, in any event, has to immunized—there are some situations that can be dangerous for your dog's health.

Eating grass: In itself, this is an entirely natural act, and it was completely safe for dogs until the contamination of fields with pesticides and herbicides. Grass that grows near such farmland is often so affected that dogs become seriously ill after eating it. Consequently, never allow your pet to eat grass growing near fields used for farming.

This Yorkshire mongrel has to be brushed every day.

Swallowing foreign bodies: Puppies are chiefly at risk here. The same rule applies to puppies and to small children: Never let little ones out of your sight for too long. Even grown dogs sometimes swallow things that do not belong in a dog's stomach or suffer from bones that have stuck in their throat or between their teeth. Symptoms of this may be choking, drooling, coughing, and vomiting.

Eating poison: Dogs may come across poison in parks and public places where it is put out to combat rats. Usually, brightly colored signs warn the public that poison has been put out. In this case, you absolutely have to put your pet on its leash. The notices also specify the type of poison used, and this information is vital if your dog really has ingested some. The veterinarian will know what antidote will—perhaps—help. The first signs of poisoning are heavy drooling, vomiting, and diarrhea, possibly mixed with blood. Go without delay to a veterinarian or to the emergency room of an animal hospital.

Snow: It conceals dangers for a dog. The animal races around, wallows in the cool wet snow, and then eats a good helping of the icy stuff. The result may be a cold and gastrointestinal problems. Do not allow your dog to eat snow, and do not throw snowballs for it to catch. Divert the animal's attention by playing ball. After the walk, towel your pet dry at home. To guard against chapped or cracked paws and to protect them from the salt used to thaw snow and ice, lubricate the dog's paws with petroleum jelly before the walk.

Biting: Every dog may at some time become involved in this. In dogs with light, short hair, wounds caused

This four-year-old child is somewhat afraid of the large dog, although the dog loves children above all else.

by bites are clearly visible at once, but in dogs with long, curly hair, even deep wounds often remain undetected. The dog's saberlike teeth can penetrate deep, and painful inflammations are the result. Check your dog carefully for injuries after every serious biting incident. If you have been allowing your pet to roam freely, you had better seriously reconsider this practice. Even if local ordinances do not require that animals be confined or kept on leash, the dangers of traffic, other animals, etc., are overwhelming. If you are not certain whether or not your pet has been bitten, take it to the veterinarian. Surgery may be required to prevent an abscess from forming.

Dogs that persist in gnawing at a wound or a bandage can be prevented from doing so by this type of hood.

You can remove ticks with tweezers.

Health Problems

Symptom	Possible Causes and Remedial Measures That You Can Take
Does not drink	Enough liquid in food
Greatly increased thirst	Overheated after romp; has eaten a great deal of dry food
Diarrhea	Too much milk, cold food, dog has eaten snow, sudden change in diet, stress
Vomiting	Dog has eaten grass, has gulped its food, heartburn
Coughing	Choking, especially from gulping water
Bad breath	Dog has eaten feces, carrion, or other foul-smelling matter
Gas (flatulence)	Predominantly meat diet, sudden change of food, does not tolerate some type of food
Straining without releasing feces or urine	Constipation resulting from lack of exercise, too much dry food and too little water, too many bones, uterine contractions
Heavy breathing	Panting while overheated, exertion or excitement

If These Symptoms Appear Too, There Is Cause for Alarm	Possible Diagnosis and Treatment by Veterinarian
Drooling, difficulty swallowing, coughing, choking	Foreign body (bone) in throat; paralysis of throat (rabies), enlargement of throat: See veterinarian at once!
Vomiting and subnormal temperature	Kidney damage (with uremia)
Apathy, staggering, subnormal temperature	Diabetes
In female: vomiting, fever, possibly vaginal discharge	Pyometra (accumulation of pus in uterus)
Blood in stools, vomiting	Worm infestation, gastrointestinal infection, liver and pancreas disorder, poisoning: See veterinarian at once!
Accompanied by whitish-yellow or bloody mucus	Gastritis, foreign body in stomach, liver or kidney disorder, poisoning: See veterinarian at once!
Dry cough with choking on phelgm	Tonsillitis, pharyngitis, or laryngitis
Dry, hacking cough with choking and some bloody phelgm	Foreign body or tumor in throat: See veterinarian at once!
Thin mucus discharge, difficulty breathing, fever	Cold, bronchitis, pneumonia (possibly distemper): See veterinarian at once!
Wet, deep cough, difficulty breathing	Cardiac defect with lung involvement (cardiac asthma), pulmonary edema: See veterinarian at once!
Drooling, perhaps mixed with blood	Tartar, periodontal disease, abscessed tooth, foreign body (bone) or tumor in mouth
Vomiting, excessive thirst, breath that smells putrid or like urine	Gastritis, serious kidney ailment with uremia
Vomiting; light, paste-like feces	Chronic pancreas or liver disorder
Especially in a large dog: choking on phlegm, abdomen bloated like balloon, complete apathy, labored breathing	Twisted stomach: See veterinarian at once; dog needs surgery within four hours!
Bloody mucus or blood discharged from anus	Intestinal blockage by bones (bone splinters in rectum): See veterinarian at once!
Bloody urine or dribbling	Stones in urethra or bladder: See veterinarian at once!
Fever, cough, sneezing	Cold, respiratory infection (kennel cough)
Deep, wet cough, tachycardia	Heart defect with lung involvement (cardiac asthma), pulmonary edema: See veterinarian at once!
Irregular breathing and abdominal straining	Lung or diaphragm rupture after an accident: See veterinarian at once!
Pale mucous membranes, tachycardia	Internal bleeding after accident or poisoning: See veterinarian at once!

Understanding Dogs

From the Wolf to the Domestic Dog

The dog (*Canis familiaris*) belongs to the large Canidae family, which also includes wolves, jackals, coyotes, and foxes. Previously, it was thought that several canine species played an important role as ancestors of the dog, but today it is believed that the wolf alone was the dog's ancestor.

One thing is certain: The friendship between humans and dogs began about 12,000 years ago. The dog is our oldest domestic animal. Keeping a dog had quite a number of advantages for humans. As an animal that lives in packs, the wolf was accustomed to taking its place in a social hierarchy. Consequently, it had the prerequisites necessary for acknowledging a human as pack leader and allowing itself to be taught and trained by such a leader. The dog, which can hear better, smell better, and run faster than a human, became an indispensable helper during the hunt. It also guarded settlements and watched over cattle.

The Origin of the Breeds

The more numerous and demanding the dog's tasks became, the more humans were forced to breed "specialists." Animals with certain traits of character and favorable physical characteristics were bred with one another until the appropriate type of dog was thought to have been found. These efforts were the beginnings of the history of breeding and the origin of almost all the dog breeds known today. Formerly, the dogs of a breed were far less uniform in appearance. It was not until the end of the previous century, when the first dog shows were held, that so-called standards were laid down. These are precise descriptions of the ideal type (appearance and nature) of a breed. Today, it is not unimportant for a dog owner to know the purpose for which the breed he has chosen was bred, or to know the various breeds from which his mongrel is descended. The information is significant because the characteristics and the body structure that have been bred into a certain breed continue to be passed on. By virtue of their inherited traits, dogs used for guarding and herding, for example—such as the collie, English sheepdog, shelty, and bearded collie—possess the ideal prerequisites for life in a family where other pets are present. They will not hunt the other pets in the house, nor will they hunt when they are outdoors. A herd dog, after all, never was allowed to leave the herd or flock. These animals also have a well-developed instinct for keeping the family— that is, their "flock"—together. Anyone who wants a docile lap dog needs

A West Highland white terrier, eight weeks old—a high-spirited, convivial dog. Like all terriers, it has to be trained with great firmness.

***Akita, two years old:** The Akita, which comes from Japan, has to be trained by someone with sensitivity and an understanding of dogs.*

this type of information as well: The Yorkshire terrier, although small and pretty, was bred to catch rats and rabbits, and it still is equipped with the often underestimated determination to achieve its own objectives that is present in all the terrier breeds.

The Love Life of Dogs

You will have to grapple with this issue, whether your pet is a purebred or a mongrel.

What You Need to Know about a Female in Heat

A female dog, or bitch, usually is ready to mate twice a year, generally in the spring and in the late fall; she is in heat, in estrus, or in season. The female comes into estrus for the first time in her life when she is sexually mature. The exact time varies greatly, depending on the breed. In some miniature breeds that mature early, a female may experience estrus when only six months old. Late developers (for the most part, large dogs) first come into season at the age of twelve months or older.

Not all dogs are in heat every six months. An interval of four to eight months may separate the phases of heat, and many dogs are ready to mate only once a year.

Phases and Course of Events

If you want to prevent a bitch from becoming pregnant, you will have to familiarize yourself with the estrual cycle and watch the course of events carefully.

The early phase lasts about ten days. There are initial indications that a heat period is about to begin. The dog becomes restless. She licks herself more frequently, and a vaginal discharge—first a clear fluid, then bloody—begins. On her walks, the bitch urinates more and entices all the males in the vicinity by means of her scent. At this point, however, she still is unreceptive to males. This changes on about the tenth day of the cycle.

During the estrual peak, which lasts approximately seven to eight days, the dog is prepared to mate. Now she looks for a suitor, stops when she sees one approaching, and bends her tail to the side. Be on the alert during this time if you do not want puppies. It is best to take the female out for only a short walk to do her business; do not let her off the leash, and do not leave her unattended, even in your own backyard. Ask owners of male dogs to put their pets on a leash.

After the peak, the heat period will come to an end. The female will continue to be quite attractive to male dogs, but she will not be receptive to their attentions.

What to Do When the Female Is Bred

As part of the procreative act, the male and the female are locked together. The penis enlarges considerably, and the vaginal muscles squeeze and hold the penis in place. The animals may remain locked for 15 to 30 minutes. Under no circumstances should you try to separate them sooner—it would be too late anyway. Pulling the animals apart by force can injure them, and it would be painful in any case.

How to Prevent Offspring

If an unplanned pregnancy occurs, it is best to take your pet to the veterinarian immediately. He can give her a hormone injection that will have an abortive effect. For reasons of health,

Floppy ears in resting position.

Listening position—dogs can turn their ears toward the source of a noise.

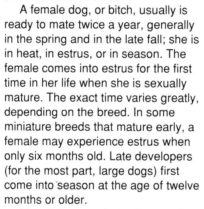

however, this option should be chosen only in a real emergency. It is preferable to consider ahead of time how to prevent your pet from becoming pregnant.

Hormone treatment administered by a veterinarian, which will prevent estrus, is possible but not recommended. Inflammations of the uterus often result.

Sterilization—that is, tubal ligation—will make conception impossible, but will not suppress all the side effects of heat or prevent the condition called false pregnancy. Consequently, it is not recommended.

The best solution is spaying, removal of the ovaries. This procedure will not impair the bitch's health; on the contrary, it will prevent uterine disorders due to old age and eliminate the possibility of pregnancy. The dog's life will be less stressful. Be sure to feed your pet slightly less, because she will tend to gain weight after being spayed.

Castration of the Male

Many dog owners and even many veterinarians are reluctant to resort to this operation, which involves removal of the male dog's testicles. Medically, there is no reason for this hesitancy; on the contrary, it is a way to avoid the prostate problems that occur with relative frequency in old age. The notion that castrated males are sluggish, about as lively as sleeping pills, also is mere prejudice. The dogs will not grow fat, either, if they are fed somewhat less. If your male dog is good-tempered and stable, there is no reason to castrate him.

If the following indications are present, however, I would recommend castration:

- increased combativeness where other males are concerned;
- persistent climbing on his owner's leg and rubbing himself;
- tendency to stray and run away; and
- if the male suffers from his unfulfilled drives so greatly that he scarcely eats and begins to lose weight.

If You Want to Raise Puppies

The saying "A female has to have at least one litter of puppies" is nonsense. If you decide to raise a litter of puppies, do not let this notion motivate you. In general, think long and hard about this decision, because raising a

During mating, the male and the female remain locked together for 15 to 30 minutes. Never forcibly separate them!

litter of young pups not only requires a great deal of experience with dogs, but also takes an enormous amount of time. You can proceed on the assumption that you will be on call constantly from the time of birth to the time the puppies go to new homes, no sooner than eight weeks later. You also should be certain that you will be able

Cute and trusting—who can resist such a look?

to find really good homes for the young dogs. If you have decided to raise pups, I recommend that you first learn as much as possible from specialized books. If breeding purebred dogs, you can consult the breeder of your bitch or the appropriate breed club.

The Dog and Its Sensory Capacities

The dog's ability to attain such great significance as a guard, hunter, or tracker also is attributable to the fact that its sensory capacities have developed so differently from those of a human.

In the World of Scents

Just as humans are "eye-minded," the dog is "nose-minded": A dog's nose provides it with the most important information about its environment. By means of its sense of smell, the dog can orient itself; it can recognize humans and other dogs by their odor; and it can "read" messages left by other dogs on trees or walls. Many of the olfactory messages that a dog sniffs out are inaccessible to our sense of smell. Nevertheless, it cannot be said that dogs have a better sense of smell than humans. A dog, for example, obviously cannot perceive the fragrance of a flower much better than humans can. Its sense of smell is almost unexcelled, however, when it comes to substances that play an important role in its own life. One such substance is butyric acid, contained in the sweat of humans and animals. A dog can smell it one million times better than a human can. Similarly, a dog can follow for a long time the track of an animal fleeing in fright. A dog's sense of smell can detect that we are afraid even before you yourself become conscious of your fear.

This refined sense of smell has made the dog an invaluable helper for mankind. Dogs used in drug searches can discover narcotics even when concealed in a gasoline tank or in bags of herbs. Specially trained avalanche search dogs can smell people buried under feet of snow, and other dogs with special training can find survivors trapped under debris even days after a disaster, just by using their noses. The best nose—belonging to a Doberman pinscher named Sour—tracked a game poacher for almost 100 miles (160 km)!

The Sense of Hearing

Dogs hear high tones in particular much better than humans do. Humans can pick up an average of 20,000 acoustic vibrations per second (kHz), whereas a dog is able to perceive between 40,000 and 100,000 vibrations. Consequently, the dog reacts, for example, to an ultrasonic whistle

that humans cannot hear at all. The animal can hear the extremely high-pitched sounds made by mice and other small animals that also are numbered among the wolf's prey.

Dogs with erect ears can move them independently of one another and point them, like funnels, precisely at the source of a sound. Just as dogs are able to commit odors to memory, they also can remember sounds. In this way, they can recognize familiar footsteps on the stairs and stand waiting at the door, wagging their tails,

Fierce—all signs point to attack.

Ears that are pricked up mean self-confidence, alertness, and readiness to be on guard.

long before the key turns in the lock. Upon hearing sounds that are inaudible for humans, a dog will give a warning, and this has made the animal indispensable as a guard.

Sight

A dog can perceive even the tiniest movements in the distance, for example, the directing hand of the shepherd, or rapidly moving objects like a fleeing rabbit. On the other hand, things that do not move are practically impossible for the dog to detect with its eyes. For this reason, many of its quarries first will stand still, as if rooted to the spot, before they make an attempt to flee.

My tip: No one, child or adult, should run away from a strange dog. It is better to stay absolutely still. Running away would be certain to arouse the dog's instinct to pursue its quarry.

How Dogs Communicate

Dogs communicate with humans and with other members of their own species in two ways: by vocal utterances and by body language.

Vocal Utterances

Dogs howl less than wolves, but they bark more. This is a result of domestication. The dog was bred to be a guard and protector whose task it is to warn against danger. Some dogs like to bark, whereas others are less "chatty." The pitch and sequence of the sounds the animal makes depend on the dog's degree of excitement, its size, and its individual manner of communication. In general, however, the following vocal utterances hold true.

Dogs bark to convey an invitation to play, a greeting, a warning, and a

sense of uneasiness. They also bark because other dogs are barking—everyone is familiar with this scenario: When one dog in the neighborhood starts to yap, all the others chime in.

Woofing is a deep sound originating in the throat, made with the dog's mouth closed. Usually this noise is heard before the dog starts to bark.

Growling—depending on the degree of excitement—is accompanied by bared teeth and hair that stands on end. It is a threatening noise directed at a human or another animal. It also may be a warning noise made by a dog when it has heard something threatening.

Howling: A long drawn-out sound made by dogs when they feel lonely or respond to certain noises—sirens, bells, music.

Squealing and uttering brief yowls are signs of distress, fear, pain, or terror.

Whimpering and whining: These sounds are derived from puppy language. Puppies express themselves in this way when they are hungry or feel

The Body Language of Dogs

Rest, relaxation   *Excitement*

lonely. Full-grown dogs makes these noises when in distress or because they have learned that they can get attention in this way.

Body Language

Even more than by making sounds, dogs communicate by their mimicry, through posture, tail position, bristled hair, and many other movements of their bodies. Many of the gestures that a dog uses to communicate with its human have their origin in the dialogue between a puppy and its mother. Here are three examples:

Offering a paw is a gesture of greeting and appeasement that a dog also makes when begging for affection or food. It lays its paw on a person's knee or holds the paw out in the air. Offering a paw is derived from the puppy's habit of pushing its paws in turn against its mother as it nurses.

Lying down on its back is a gesture of submission as well as trust. If, during an altercation with other dogs, your pet throws itself down on its back or its side, puts its tail between its legs in fear, lays its ears back, and displays its unprotected belly, it is saying this: "I surrender. Please don't hurt me." This pattern of behavior is learned while the dog is still a puppy, playing with its littermates. If, while relaxed and content, your dog rolls on its back, perhaps waving its front paws as well, this means: "Please scratch me." The grown dog's pleasure in having its chest or belly scratched also originated in its experiences as a puppy. A mother dog rolls her puppies on their backs so she can lap their bellies to stimulate a bowel movement, which she then eats in order to keep the bedding clean. This gives the puppies a luxurious sense of being cared for, a feeling the mature animal seeks to reexperience with its human.

Jumping up and licking faces: Even if you like this behavior, most people feel completely unenthusiastic about being jumped on and licked. Consequently, forbid your dog in good time to behave in this way, without destroying the animal's pleasure in welcoming you (see page 27).

Ears laid back at the sides are a sign of insecurity or fearfulness. Accompanied by bristling of the dog's fur and growling or snarling, this indicates readiness to attack.

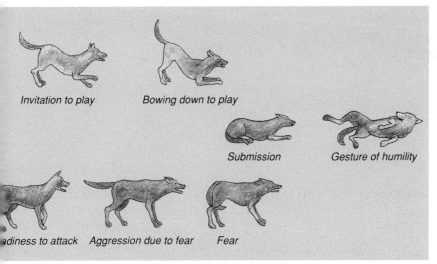

Invitation to play

Bowing down to play

Submission

Gesture of humility

...diness to attack   *Aggression due to fear*   *Fear*

59

Useful Addresses and Recommended Reading

For Information and Printed Materials

American Society for the Prevention of Cruelty of Animals (ASPCA)
441 East 92nd Street
New York, New York 10028

American Veterinary Medical Association
930 North Meacham Road
Schaumberg, Illinois 60173

Canine Eye Registration Foundation
South Campus Court,
Building C
Purdue University
West Lafayette, Indiana 47907

Humane Society of the United States
2100 L Street N.W.
Washington, D.C. 20037

Orthopedic Foundation for Animals
2300 Nifong Boulevard
Columbia, Missouri 65201

Therapy Dogs International
P.O. Box 2796
Cheyenne, Wyoming 82003

International Kennel Clubs

The American Kennel Club (AKC)
51 Madison Avenue
New York, New York 10038

United Kennel Club
100 East Kilgore Road
Kalamazoo, Michigan 49001-5598

The Kennel Club
1-4 Clargis Street Picadilly
London W7Y 8AB
England

Canadian Kennel Club
111 Eglington Avenue
Toronto 12, Ontario
Canada

Australian National Kennel Council
Royal Show Grounds
Ascot Vale
Victoria
Australia

Irish Kennel Club
41 Harcourt Street
Dublin 2
Ireland

New Zealand Kennel Club
P.O. Box 523
Wellington, 1
New Zealand

Books

In addition to the most recent edition of the official publication of the AKC, *The Complete Dog Book* published by Howell Book House, Inc. in New York, there are:

Alderton, David. *The Dog Care Manual*. Barron's Educational Series, Inc., Hauppauge, New York, 1986.

Baer, Ted. *Communicating with Your Dog*. Barron's Educational Series, Inc., Hauppauge, New York, 1989.

—*How to Teach Your Old Dog New Tricks*. Barron's Educational Series, Inc., Hauppauge, New York, 1991.

Frye, Fredric. *First Aid for Your Dog*. Barron's Educational Series, Inc., Hauppauge, New York, 1987.

Klever, Ulrich. *The Complete Book of Dog Care*. Barron's Educational Series, Inc., Hauppauge, New York, 1989.

Lorenz, Konrad Z. *Man Meets Dog*. Penguin Books, London and New York, 1967.

Pinney, Christopher. *Guide to Home Pet Grooming*. Barron's Educational Series, Inc., Hauppauge, New York, 1990.

Smythe, Reginald H. *The Mind of the Dog*. Thomas, Bannerstone House, London, Great Britain, 1961.

Ullmann, Hans-J. *The New Dog Handbook*. Barron's Educational Series, Inc. Hauppauge, New York, 1985.

Index

Page references in **boldface** type indicate color photos. **C1** indicates front cover; **C2**, inside front cover; **C3**, inside back cover; **C4**, back cover.

Acknowledgment
The author and the publisher are grateful to Dr. Uwe Streiferd for checking the chapter "Prevention and Diseases" and for compiling the table "Health Problems."

Translated from the German by Kathleen Luft.

Photographer and Author
Monika Wegler is the author and photographer of several of Barron's successful Pet Owner's Manuals. She has worked for many years as a photojournalist for the specialized magazine *Das Tier* (*The Animal*) and for other German and international publications. Her areas of specialization are the keeping, care, breeding, and behavior of dogs, cats, and rabbits.

The color photos on the covers:
Front cover: English sheepdogs. Inside front cover: A chow chow and a Bernese mountain dog are the parents of this four-month-old mongrel. Back cover: Airedale terrier.

English translation © 1992 by Barron's Educational Series, Inc.

© Copyright 1991 by Gräfe und Unzer Verlag GmbH, Munich, Germany.
The title of the German book is *Hunde.*

Translated from the German by Kathleen Luft.

All inquiries should be addressed to:
Barron's Educational Series, Inc.
250 Wireless Boulevard
Hauppauge, New York 11788

Library of Congress Catalog Card No. 92-5794

International Standard Book No. 0-8120-4822-9

Library of Congress Cataloging-in-Publication Data

Wegler, Monika.
[Hunde. English]
Dogs : how to take care of them and understand them / Monika Wegler; with color photographs by Monika Wegler and drawings by György Jankovics.
p. cm.
Translation of: Hunde.
Includes index.
ISBN 0-8120-4822-9
1. Dogs. I. Title.
SF427.W3813   1992
636.7'0887—dc20   92-5794
                                                    CIP

PRINTED IN HONG KONG
2345   9955   98765432

Important Note
Barron's Pet Owner's Manual *Dogs* deals with the acquisition and keeping of dogs. The author and the publisher consider it important to point out that the rules of dog keeping set forth in this book apply primarily to normally developed young dogs from a good breeder, that is, to healthy animals with good character traits.

Anyone who takes a full-grown dog into his or her care has to be aware that the animal already has been molded to a great extent by its association with other people. Observe such a dog carefully and watch how it behaves with humans; take a look at the previous owner as well. If the dog comes from an animal shelter, the personnel there may be able to give you information about the animal's origin and characteristics. Owing to bad experiences with humans, some dogs may have peculiar behavior or may tend to bite. These dogs should be taken in only by experienced dog owners. Even well-trained and carefully supervised dogs may cause damage to someone else's property or even cause accidents. Sufficient insurance coverage is in your own interest. In any case, I strongly recommend taking out a dog liability policy for your pet.

Large Dogs

Airedale terriers

English sheepdogs: male and female

Irish setter

Siberian husky

Collie (right) and two shelties